NORTH AMERICAN
cranes

NORTH AMERICAN
cranes

by Lesley A. DuTemple

A Carolrhoda Nature Watch Book

Carolrhoda Books, Inc. / Minneapolis

To Christopher—my son, my love, and a
great bird-watching buddy. —L.A.D.

The author and publisher wish to thank Dr. Rod
Drewien, University of Idaho, for his help in the
preparation of this book.

Carolrhoda Books, Inc., c/o The Lerner Publishing Group
241 First Avenue North, Minneapolis, MN 55401 U.S.A.

Website address: www.lernerbooks.com

LIBRARY OF CONGRESS CATALOGING-IN-PUBLICATION DATA

DuTemple, Lesley A.
    North American cranes / by Lesley A. DuTemple.
      p.   cm.
    "A Carolrhoda nature watch book."
    Includes index.
    Summary: Describes the physical characteristics, diet,
natural habitat, and life cycle of these large wading
birds, and tells about the efforts of scientists to establish
resident flocks.
    ISBN 1-57505-302-0
    1. Whooping crane—Juvenile literature. 2. Sandhill
crane—Juvenile literature. 3. Wildlife reintroduction—
North America—Juvenile literature. [1. Whooping crane.
2. Sandhill crane. 3. Wildlife reintroduction. 4. Cranes
(Birds)] I. Title.
QL696.G84D88 1999
598.3'2—dc21   98-4519

Manufactured in the United States of America
1 2 3 4 5 6 – JR – 04 03 02 01 00 99

CONTENTS

An Ancient Ritual   7
Physical Characteristics and Diet   10
Migration   17
Wintering and Nesting Grounds   23
The Life of a Chick   29
Sandhills Helping Whoopers   33
Establishing New Flocks and
    Protecting Old Habitats   42
Glossary   46
Index   47

AN ANCIENT RITUAL

Gar-ooo! GAR-OOO! Gar-ooo-OOO!
As the trumpeting call echoes across the frozen marsh, a snowshoe hare stops its nibbling and sniffs the still air. Deep in the woods, a fox pricks up its ears.

GAR-OOO! GAR-OOO! GAR-OOO! The call rings out again and again, echoing off the surrounding hills.

Heavy frost covers the landscape. Thin sheets of ice fringe the edges of shallow ponds. In the shadow of black spruce trees, crusty patches of snow still linger. Spring has come to the subarctic—the land surrounding the Arctic Circle—and the cranes are arriving.

The morning sun clears the bare tree-tops and spotlights two cranes as they circle over the marsh. Calling to each other, they circle lower, their enormous wings beating the frozen air. Lower and lower they come, until their long, slender legs touch the ground with a soft thud. Flapping their wings, they run across the ground and come to a stop several feet away. The larger crane straightens his long neck and ruffles his feathers into place. The smaller crane quickly darts her eyes around the marsh.

The cranes have returned to their nesting grounds.

When cranes return to their nesting area each spring, they are doing more than just returning from a balmy winter break. The cranes are performing a ritual that's thousands of years old. That's how long cranes have been on Earth, and that's how long they've been returning to their nesting spots.

The first bird, archaeopteryx, evolved about 150 million years ago—back when dinosaurs roamed the earth. Scientists think that the archaeopteryx descended from a small reptile that made its way up into the trees as a matter of survival.

Archaeopteryx, which means "ancient wing," was a crow-sized creature with feathers covering its entire body. Feathers are actually extended reptile scales, and archaeopteryx still looked a lot like a reptile. Toes and claws extended from its wings. But a reptile's body temperature is controlled from outside its body— when it's warm outside, a reptile's body temperature rises, and when it's cold outside, a reptile's body temperature falls. The archaeopteryx, on the other hand, was warm-blooded, meaning no matter what the temperature is outside, the animal's body temperature stays the same. This is true of all modern birds.

The archaeopteryx could also grasp branches with its feet. It was not able to fly for long distances, but it could probably glide from branch to branch.

Archaeopteryx became **extinct,** or died out, at the same time as dinosaurs—about 65 million years ago. At that time, the ancestors of modern birds, including cranes, first appeared. These birds looked more like modern birds than the archaeopteryx ever did.

Modern cranes are members of the family Gruidae. There are 15 **species,** or kinds, of cranes found in the world. Cranes can be found on every continent except South America and Antarctica. Two crane species are found in North America: the sandhill crane, *Grus canadensis,* and the whooping crane, *Grus americana.*

The archaeopteryx (left) *died out with the dinosaurs, at about the time the ancestors of cranes appeared. There are 15 species of modern cranes found around the world, including the blue crane* (top right) *and the crowned crane* (bottom right), *both of which can be found in Africa.*

PHYSICAL CHARACTERISTICS AND DIET

Crane species differ in size and coloration, but all cranes have several things in common. Cranes are large wading birds. Wading birds, such as flamingos and herons, wade in shallow waters in search of food. All crane species have long, slender legs, unwebbed feet, long necks, and powerful, pointed beaks. Male and female cranes of the same species look alike, although the male is usually larger than the female. All crane species mate for life, and both males and females help care for their young. All crane species have loud, powerful voices that can be heard more than 1 mile (1.6 km) away.

Sandhill cranes, or "sandhills," are the most numerous cranes in North America. They're even the most numerous cranes in the world. There are over 500,000 sandhill cranes in North America.

Sandhills are divided into six subspecies. They are the lesser, Canadian, Cuban, Florida, Mississippi, and greater sandhill cranes. Size is the greatest difference between them. The lesser sandhill crane is the smallest, but it is still large and striking in appearance. An adult stands about 3 feet tall (0.9 m), and it weighs between 6 and 8 pounds (2.7–3.6 kg). That's about as tall as a first grader, but only about the weight of a house cat! It has a wingspan of up to 5.5 feet (1.7 m). The greater sandhill is the largest. An adult greater sandhill crane stands about 4.5 feet tall (1.4 m), and it weighs between 10 and 14 pounds (4.5–6.4 kg)—or about as tall as a fourth grader and as heavy as a bowling ball. Its wingspan can extend to 6.5 feet (2 m).

Left: *Both male and female cranes help care for their young.*
Right: *A sandhill crane wades in shallow water.*

One reason cranes stand so tall is because of their long legs and necks. A greater sandhill's legs may be nearly 2 feet long (0.6 m), and their necks may be 18 to 20 inches long (46–51 cm).

Sandhills are large cranes, but whooping cranes are even larger. They're the tallest birds in North America. Adult whooping cranes, or "whoopers," stand nearly 5 feet tall (1.5 m), weigh between 13 and 16 pounds (5.9–7.3 kg), and have a wingspan that can reach up to 7.5 feet (2.3 m).

Whooping cranes are taller than any bird in North America.

Sandhills stain their feathers during preening. Some sandhills stain themselves a lot (left), *and other sandhills stain their feathers just a little* (above).

Unlike some water birds, cranes do not have webbed feet. Their feet are designed to wade and walk through mud. Three large "toes" spread apart as they walk. These toes, along with a tiny back toe located a little farther up the leg, help keep them from sinking. Cranes' long legs allow them to wade through shallow water as they look for food.

Sandhill cranes are mostly covered with pale gray **plumage,** or feathers. Some sandhills have white plumage on their throat and dark tips on their wing feathers. To keep their feathers smooth, sandhills—like all birds—**preen.** The cranes rub their beaks near the base of their tails, where a small gland that contains waterproofing oil is located. Then they rub their beaks over their feathers to separate and smooth each feather. A small amount of the waterproofing oil coats the cranes' feathers as they preen.

13

During the spring and summer months, sandhills stain their feathers a rusty brown color. When sandhills preen, they dip their beaks in the mud. Ferric oxide, or rust, from the mud, stains the feathers. Some sandhills stain themselves so heavily that their feathers turn a brick red color. Biologists believe that sandhills stain their feathers on purpose, perhaps to camouflage, or disguise, themselves from enemies during the mating season.

The adult whooper's plumage is pure white with black facial markings and black wingtips. The black wingtips can only be seen when the bird is flying, however. Whoopers also preen, but they do not stain themselves with ferric oxide as sandhills do.

Whooping cranes do not stain their feathers when they preen—they keep their feathers white.

14

A sandhill crane

A whooping crane

A whooper's head is a bit larger than a sandhill's. Both species have yellow or orange eyes and dark gray beaks. A sandhill's beak can grow up to 6 inches long (15 cm). A whooper's beak is slightly longer and more powerful than a sandhill's. But it is the top of a crane's head that most people notice. Both sandhills and whoopers have a patch of skin with no feathers on their head—and it's red!

Whooper and sandhill cranes are **omnivorous.** That means they'll eat both plants and animals. Their diet consists of insects, fish, berries, crabs, plants, grains, or even other birds. Sandhills prefer grains, such as corn or barley. They also eat seeds and tubers. Whoopers prefer crabs and other small animals. But all cranes are opportunistic feeders—if they see an opportunity to eat something, they will.

Sometimes a bobcat, coyote, wolf, or golden eagle will kill a young or sick bird. On a rare occasion, a **predator,** or animal that eats other animals, may even kill an adult crane. But usually, adult cranes do not need to worry about predators. The cranes' large bodies and powerful beaks keep most predators away.

Cranes need an abundant supply of food. An adult sandhill can easily eat a pound of grain a day. So unless they're being fed (by farmers or in a wildlife refuge), this means that cranes need a lot of space. In the wild, one pair of cranes can use up to 300 acres of land to find enough food.

Bobcats are one of the few crane enemies.

Cranes eat both fish and grains.

MIGRATION

As large animals that eat almost anything, sandhill and whooping cranes should be able to live anywhere, or so you would think. But cranes live in specific **habitats,** or areas in which they live. All cranes need habitats that include **wetlands.** Wetlands are areas, such as marshes, where there is more water than dry land.

A few crane species stay in the same place all year long. The Cuban, Florida, and Mississippi sandhill cranes live in wetland areas in the Caribbean and in the southeastern part of the United States.

17

Most cranes have two homes—nesting grounds in the north and wintering grounds in the south. They always fly the same route between these homes.

But most whoopers and sandhills **migrate.** They travel to a new home when the seasons change. By late fall, migrating cranes begin to arrive at their wintering grounds, wetland areas in the southern United States and northern Mexico. During the spring and summer, cranes live at their nesting grounds near the Arctic Circle, in the northern United States, and in eastern Siberia. Some whoopers and sandhills nest in marshes surrounded by forests and marshy lakes. But a large number of sandhills live on the **tundra,** a treeless area, located in the far north, with many lakes and meadows.

By late September, the cranes get rest-less. Biologists think the birds are responding to the shorter days, cooler temperatures, and diminishing food sources. The cranes wait for a good, stiff breeze to take off. Whoopers fly in small groups of two or three birds. Sandhills may start in small groups, but they join together in larger groups once they're in flight. Soon the cranes are on their way south to their wintering grounds, following a **flyway,** or route, that cranes have used for centuries.

Migrating cranes can fly more than 100 miles (161 km) in a day, sometimes up to 300 miles (483 km). Some cranes have long migration routes. They journey more than 2,500 miles (4,025 km)—twice a year!

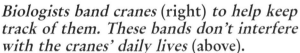

Biologists band cranes (right) *to help keep track of them. These bands don't interfere with the cranes' daily lives* (above).

To learn more about cranes and how they migrate, biologists in the 1970s began to **band** the birds. A band is an identification tag that helps biologists keep track of birds. When biologists band a bird, they attach a lightweight metal or plastic band around its leg. Bands don't hurt the crane or interfere with its flying. Some bands have a small radio transmitter on them. This transmitter sends out a signal that tells biologists where the crane is. Radio bands have helped biologists learn a lot about crane migrations.

Along their flyways, cranes need wetlands so that they can rest and feed during migration.

In 1981 and 1982, biologists followed four whooping crane families with radio transmitters. Even traveling 100 miles a day (161 km), crane migration takes many days. One family took 31 days to fly from near the Arctic Circle to the Gulf of Mexico. They traveled during 17 of those days, and they rested and fed on the other 14 days. Whenever the cranes landed, biologists noted their location and the kinds of food they ate.

Biologists found that cranes usually stopped at wetlands. But in recent years, wetlands have been destroyed and drained to make way for farms, roads, homes, and businesses. By studying the places where cranes stop, rest, and feed, biologists can identify wetlands along a flyway that need to be kept "wild and wet" for birds. It is up to people and organizations to protect the wetlands for cranes and other migrating birds.

From banding, biologists have also learned that different sandhill crane populations, or groups that fly together, use different flyways. There is only one major remaining wild whooping crane group and flyway, however. This group shares its flyway with sandhill groups. They use a flyway that goes across Canada, the Dakotas, Nebraska, and Kansas. They winter near the gulf coast of Texas, in or near the Aransas National Wildlife Refuge (NWR).

Migrating sandhills fly in many different groups. About 3,000 sandhills, along with a handful of whoopers that biologists introduced to the group, nest at the Grays Lake NWR in Idaho. This group uses a flyway that starts in Idaho, goes across southwestern Wyoming to Colorado, and ends at Bosque del Apache NWR in New Mexico. Another small group uses a flyway from the Pacific Northwest to California, while another flies between the Great Lakes and Florida.

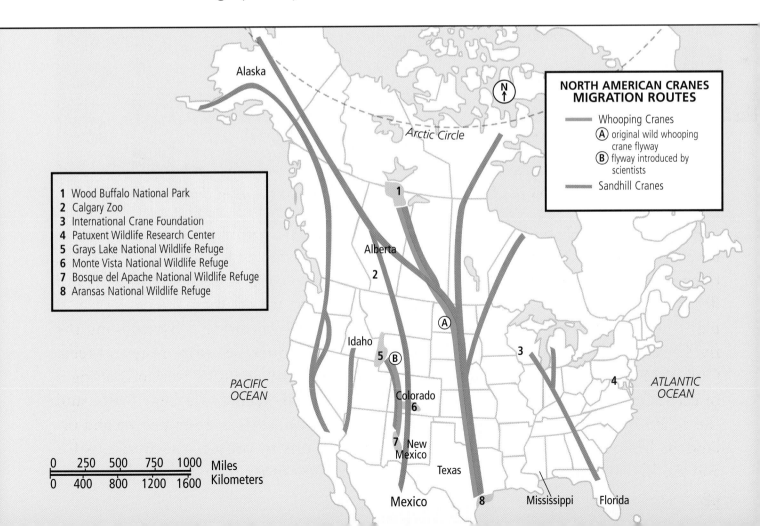

Cranes prefer to fly during the day.

Most of the time, sandhills and whoopers fly only during daylight hours. Although some migrating birds fly at night, cranes prefer to find a resting place each night during their migration. They may rest and eat for several days in one place if the food supply is plentiful.

Whoopers and sandhills usually fly at about 1,500 feet (457 m), but they can go as high as 14,000 feet (4,267 m) when flying over high mountains. That's as high as some low-flying planes. If it weren't for their loud trumpeting calls, they'd pass overhead without anyone knowing. But it's hard to ignore the loud "GAR-OOO-OOO" that cranes make—even if you can't see them!

Biologists have learned that many different species of birds use the same flyway at the same time. Snow geese, ducks, and other birds use the same flyway as the whoopers and sandhills. Thousands of birds, representing nearly 300 other bird species, share the Aransas and Bosque del Apache wintering grounds with North American cranes.

At their wintering grounds, sandhills gather in large flocks (below) while whoopers split into small family groups *(right).*

WINTERING AND NESTING GROUNDS

By November, most migrating cranes have arrived at their southern wintering grounds. Sandhills gather in large **flocks,** or groups of birds that live together. Whoopers, however, split up to live in small family groups.

The first thing whooping cranes do is claim their winter **territory,** or area in which a family of cranes choose to live. Whooper families are very territorial. They not only return to the same nesting and wintering grounds year after year—

they also return to the same territory within those grounds. They will vigorously chase away anything that comes within their chosen space.

Many whooper families claim a territory of over 200 acres (81 ha), but territories can be larger than 2,000 acres (810 ha). Whooper families consist of a chick—a crane under one year old—and its parents. Young adult cranes—cranes under 5 years old—form small flocks and live around the edges of claimed territories.

The male is the primary defender of a territory. When an unwanted visitor enters the family's territory, the male lets out a loud call and chases off the intruder. Cranes are loud! The longer a bird's **trachea,** or windpipe, the louder its voice can be. Whoopers have long, long tracheas with trumpetlike coils in them. These coiled tracheas amplify their voices so much that whoopers can be heard long before you see them. The trachea of a whooping crane is nearly 52 inches (132 cm)—about as long as the bird itself.

When the female crane hears the male, she often joins in. When a pair of cranes are defending their territory, they give a unison call. Whoopers and male sandhills point their beaks upward, while female sandhills hold their beaks horizontally. In the unison call of whoopers, the male emits two long notes, and the female joins in with three higher, shorter notes. The whoopers may repeat this duet until the intruder leaves.

The whooper male spends most of his time defending the territory, while the female spends most of her time protecting the chick and teaching it how to find food. They will, however, help each other out from time to time.

Whoopers and sandhills stay on their wintering grounds until March or April. Then they become restless again. One fine spring day, when the wind is right, they take off. They're on the move again, migrating north to their nesting grounds.

A male sandhill points his beak upward and a female sandhill holds her beak horizontally to perform a unison call.

A crane family uses the same flyway whenever it migrates. The difference between the spring and fall migrations in whoopers is the time in which the cranes take to fly. Whoopers make fewer stops in the spring—sometimes they make it to northern Canada in only 2 weeks. They need to reach the nesting grounds with enough time to build a nest, lay two eggs, and raise their chicks before it's time to head back to their wintering grounds.

Both migrating sandhills and whoopers live in small family groups at their nesting grounds. After arriving, the cranes first claim, or reclaim, their territory—just as the whoopers did at their wintering grounds. After boundaries are re-established, there's more to do than just settle down and eat . . . there's dancing to be done!

At their nesting grounds, both sandhills and whoopers live in small family groups.

One reason people find cranes so fascinating is that they dance. They dance by themselves, they dance with other cranes—they have even danced with humans! Cranes dance throughout the year. But when they finish the spring migration and reach their northern nesting grounds, the time spent dancing increases.

A crane dance begins with one bird bowing its head and flapping its wings. Then the bird leaps into the air with stiff legs, throwing its head back and skyward. Its mate responds by running toward the bird, bowing its head, and flapping its wings. Both birds jump high into the air with arched necks and stiff legs. The crane dance may continue for several minutes.

People once thought that the only time cranes danced was when they were mating. Biologists don't know all the reasons why cranes dance, but they do know that cranes dance even when they're not engaged in mating rituals. Biologists also know that cranes of all ages dance: chicks who are too young to fly, young birds, and older, established pairs.

Sometimes people might think they're watching a crane dance, but they're really seeing a crane fight. Just as they do when they dance, cranes spread their wings and jump high into the air when they fight with each other. Although the movements may look similar, hissing noises heard at the event would indicate a crane fight is taking place!

Sandhill cranes spread their wings and leap high into the air both when they're performing the crane dance and when they're fighting.

Cranes build tall nests to keep their eggs dry.

After the cranes have danced and chosen or reaffirmed a mate, they choose a nest site within their territory. Each pair builds a tall mound—sometimes 2 feet tall (0.6 m)—from bulrushes, sticks, cattails, and other plants. Because cranes live in marshes and other wetland areas, most nests are built in shallow ponds, where the water is only about 1 foot deep (0.3 m). Each nest extends about 6 to 15 inches (15–38 cm) above the water.

Female cranes do not produce eggs until they are 4 to 5 years old. Once they are old enough, females usually lay two eggs every spring. Both whooper and sandhill eggs are a little less than 4 inches long (10 cm) and weigh between 5 and 7 ounces (142–198 g). The oval eggs are cream-colored and sprinkled with brown spots.

Cranes turn (above) *and incubate* (right)
their eggs until the eggs are ready to hatch.

After the eggs are laid, both cranes take turns **incubating** the eggs, or sitting on them to keep them warm and dry. The female usually does more incubating than the male, however. They turn the eggs every day. This keeps the developing chicks from sticking to their shells.

After 29 to 31 days, a small peeping sound is heard coming from inside the shell. Hour by hour, the peeping grows louder. A new crane is about to hatch.

THE LIFE OF A CHICK

When a crane chick first hatches, it's just a little ball of wet fluff. Smaller than a robin, it weighs less than 5 ounces (142 g). There's nothing to indicate the large, graceful bird it will become.

Breaking out of an eggshell is hard work. All baby birds have an **egg tooth,** or sharp structure, on the end of their beak to help them. Inside the egg, the chick uses the egg tooth to **pip,** or tap, at the shell until it breaks. Pipping can take from 10 to 25 hours before the chick breaks free of the shell and hatches. The crane parents might use their own beaks to turn the egg a bit, but they don't help the chick hatch. A few days after hatching, the egg tooth falls off.

Chicks hatch with their eyes open. The chicks can walk shortly after their feathers dry, usually within 12 hours. At 2 to 3 days old, whooper and sandhill chicks look almost identical. Both are covered with tan-colored, fuzzy down feathers.

This crane chick recently hatched from its shell. The white tip at the end of its bill is the egg tooth.

For the first 2 or 3 days of a chick's life, its parents take turns **brooding,** or keeping the chick warm and dry. One parent sits on the nest to warm the chick. The other parent searches for food—both for itself and the chick. Soon, the newly hatched chicks learn to eat the insects their parents bring them.

29

Although female cranes usually lay two eggs, most crane pairs can only raise one chick. Only 15 to 35 percent of all sandhills are seen with two chicks. Whooping cranes virtually never raise more than one chick at a time. Both eggs normally hatch, but the most aggressive chick often gets all the food and attention. Sometimes the more aggressive chick will chase the other chick away. With less protection and less food, it soon dies.

The family uses the nest at night for the next week or two. Then they abandon the nest and spend the rest of the summer wandering through their territory to feed on insects, berries, small animals, and other foods they find. For several months, the parents will continue to provide the chick with some of its food. As the chick gradually learns to find its own food, the parents provide less and less food for the chick. By the end of the summer, the chick will find all its own food, although it may still occasionally pester its parents to feed it.

Crane chicks are able to swim just 24 hours after hatching.

This young crane chick has lost its down feathers and replaced them with cinnamon-colored feathers. It still occasionally looks to its parents for help in finding food.

At 8 weeks, a crane chick is almost as tall as its parents. It has the height and elegance of an adult crane, but with its soft head feathers, the chick still looks like a baby. You can also tell a baby from an adult by its voice. Instead of a loud trumpeting call, a chick makes a little peeping whistle, much like a baby chicken.

The chicks have learned to fly, but they're not very good at it. Flying is hard work. Crane chicks do a lot of flapping—and crashing—into bushes!

By 10 weeks, crane chicks have lost their down and have grown their first set of real feathers. Both whooper and sandhill chicks grow cinnamon- or brownish-colored feathers as they lose their baby down. Over the course of 14 months, sandhill cranes slowly develop pale gray feathers, and whooping cranes develop their brilliant white adult plumage.

All summer, adult cranes devote their energy and attention to raising their chick. Cranes are very protective parents. Any potential predator that comes near is chased away with loud alarm calls and threatening charges with sharp, jabbing beaks.

By the time the first frost hits, the young crane is almost ready to make the long journey south to the wintering grounds. The chick is now 4 to 5 months old. One crisp fall day, a stiff breeze will blow through the marsh, and the crane family will take off. Within a few weeks, nearly all the crane families will have left the nesting grounds. The migration cycle has begun again.

A young crane is nearly ready to make the long journey to its wintering grounds.

SANDHILLS HELPING WHOOPERS

Whooping cranes are the tallest birds in North America, but they have another distinguishing trait: they are the most **endangered** crane species in the world.

The whooping crane population was never very large. Before Europeans came to North America, the population was possibly about 5,000 birds. By the 1930s, cities across America were rapidly expanding. Farmers plowed the land to grow crops. Wetlands were modified and sometimes destroyed. In addition, whoopers were hunted for food. As a result, the magnificent whooping crane almost disappeared.

Biologists wanted to save the remaining whoopers. The biologists knew that the cranes spent a few winter months on the gulf coast of Texas. In 1937, the United States government made the whoopers' Texas wintering grounds into the Aransas National Wildlife Refuge, to help protect whooping cranes.

Expanding cities and new developments continue to destroy wetland areas.

At one time there were only 22 whooping cranes in North America.

Even with protected wintering grounds, whooping crane numbers were dropping. By 1941, there were only 22 birds left in North America: 16 whoopers wintered in Texas and 6 wintered in Louisiana. The Louisiana birds vanished by 1950.

In addition, the whoopers faced another problem: little variation in the species. An animal is made up of cells. Each cell contains **genes.** Genes determine an animal's ability to fight disease, its appearance, and its personality. These genes are passed on to an animal from its parents.

Each species is made up of a collection of genes, called a **gene pool.** When the gene pool is very large—with many individuals—the species has a good chance of success. There is a better chance that at least some of the species could fight a disease or adapt to a change in the environment. These survivors would then mate, produce more offspring, and add new genes to the gene pool. But when a species has only a few individuals, as the whooping crane did in 1941 with just 16 birds in Texas, the offspring comes from a very small gene pool. When there is no variation to the genes, the species can quickly become extinct, or die out, from disease or a change in the environment.

A fire-fighting helicopter pilot discovered a wild whooping crane family at Wood Buffalo National Park, located in Canada.

Although biologists couldn't increase the whoopers' gene pool, they could help preserve their habitat. But so far, they knew only where the birds were in winter. What about the rest of the year? Where were the nesting grounds and migration flyway?

In 1945, the Canadian government launched a nationwide search to find the nesting grounds of the remaining whooping cranes. For 3 years, they searched many areas of Canada by air. They found nothing. Biologists were forced to call off the search.

Then in 1954, a fire-fighting helicopter pilot was patrolling a fire in the Wood Buffalo National Park, in Canada. A flash of white caught his attention. He flew lower. There, in the marsh below, were two adult whooping cranes. With them was a chick. The nesting grounds had been found!

With this discovery, biologists could also determine the birds' flyway. From Canada to Texas, the whoopers would be protected. By 1960, the whooping crane population had increased from 16 to 36. But that number was still dangerously low. What else could biologists do to save the birds from extinction?

Biologists knew that both whooping and sandhill cranes usually laid two eggs but normally raised only one chick. In 1967, American and Canadian biologists began a **captive breeding** program—they raised chicks in laboratories. The biologists flew to Wood Buffalo National Park and removed one egg from whooping crane nests that held two eggs. The eggs were carefully transported to the Patuxent Wildlife Research Center in Laurel, Maryland, and raised in captivity.

Raising whooper chicks at Patuxent wasn't easy, but after many years of practice and experience, it became more and more successful. Over time, most of the chicks that hatched at the center survived and grew to adults.

Biologists removed one whooping crane egg from two-egg nests (left) *and carefully shipped the collected eggs* (below) *to a research center in Maryland.*

More recently, other captive breeding programs have been established at the International Crane Foundation in Baraboo, Wisconsin, and at the Calgary Zoo, in Alberta, Canada. Biologists have been encouraged by the results, but not entirely satisfied. True, they have whoopers. But they are captive whoopers. Biologists want whoopers who can survive in the wild.

For years, the Patuxent biologists had been working with the greater sandhill crane, which was not endangered, to find ways to raise endangered cranes in captivity. At the Patuxent Center, greater sandhill cranes were used to incubate whooping crane eggs. Sandhills were also used as foster parents for whooper chicks. Biologists wondered: Could wild sandhills be tricked into raising whooping crane chicks in the wild? Could sandhills teach whoopers how to live successfully in the wild?

These questions were first asked in the 1950s by Dr. Fred Bard, a Canadian biologist. In the mid-1970s, Dr. Rod Drewien, a biologist studying the Grays Lake sandhill crane flock, decided to put these questions to the test. Because he had banded many sandhills, Dr. Drewien knew a lot about the flock, including their migration route. A safe migration route for the whooper chicks was critical.

The whooping cranes' natural flyway is more than 2,500 miles long (4,023 km). Along this flyway, whoopers face the dangers of power lines, predators, airports, hunters, snowstorms, and sleet—in addition to vanishing wetlands.

But the sandhill cranes at Grays Lake, Idaho, migrate only 850 miles (1,368 km). Along the way, Monte Vista NWR provides a resting spot. The sandhills winter at Bosque del Apache NWR in New Mexico. Sandhill cranes hatched at Grays Lake spend most of their lives on protected lands.

Whooper eggs replaced sandhill eggs for some of the Grays Lake sandhills. In this picture (right) *a whooper egg and a sandhill egg sit side-by-side on a sandhill nest. A whooper chick* (above) *hatches in Grays Lake. Its foster sandhill parents will raise it to be part of the Grays Lake sandhill flock.*

In May 1975, the Canadian and U.S. governments began a daring experiment with sandhill parents and whooper eggs. Fourteen whooping crane eggs were removed from two-egg nests in Wood Buffalo and flown to Grays Lake. Dr. Drewien and other biologists were going to attempt to establish a second wild whooping crane flock.

In Grays Lake the biologists replaced sandhill eggs with whooper eggs. The removed sandhill crane eggs were sent to the Patuxent Center and hatched. To be foster parents, a sandhill couple had to have been consistently successful in raising young for several years.

The wild sandhills turned out to be good foster parents. The whooper chicks were well cared for and accepted by the entire flock. Four whooper chicks survived that first year.

From 1975 through 1988, whooping crane eggs from the Wood Buffalo nesting grounds and from the Patuxent Center were placed in the nests of sandhill foster parents, and the chicks were raised as part of the Grays Lake greater sandhill crane flock. In 1988, when biologists abandoned the program, about 20 whooping cranes lived with the Grays Lake flock. By the fall of 1997, only three were left. One of these was a crane hatched in 1982. The other two cranes hatched in 1983 and 1984.

A foster sandhill crane couple looks for food with its whooper chick in Grays Lake, Idaho.

There were several reasons to abandon the project. One reason was that the whooping cranes did not breed with each other. Biologists speculated that perhaps the whoopers couldn't find each other among the thousands of sandhills. Or worse, maybe the whoopers thought they *were* sandhills.

Most important, more whooping cranes died than survived. The cranes were dying from disease caused by overcrowded conditions at their wintering grounds. With vanishing wetlands, more and more birds have to crowd into smaller spaces. Avian cholera and avian tuberculosis are just two of the deadly diseases that strike birds when they're overcrowded.

The Grays Lake nesting grounds aren't overcrowded, but the Bosque del Apache wintering grounds are home to thousands of birds. When the snow goose population is high, the danger of an outbreak of cholera or tuberculosis increases. Both these diseases pass easily from geese to cranes. In addition to disease, the whoopers were dying during migration. Some were lost, others collided with power lines, and a few were attacked by golden eagles.

Biologists needed a new plan. They began to look for a place to establish a **resident flock** of wild whooping cranes. Resident flocks—such as the Cuban, Florida, and Mississippi sandhill cranes that live in the Caribbean and in the southeastern United States—do not migrate. They stay in the same area all year long. Resident flocks are exposed to fewer hazards than migrating flocks. Resident flocks also stay by themselves, so the risk of avian cholera and tuberculosis is much lower.

At Bosque del Apache NWR, thousands of birds—including North American cranes and snow geese—make their homes.

Biologists knew that there had once been a resident whooping crane flock in Louisiana, but it had vanished by 1950. Maybe they could re-establish a resident flock of whoopers in the southeastern part of the United States.

Power lines sometimes kill cranes and other migrating birds.

ESTABLISHING NEW FLOCKS AND PROTECTING OLD HABITATS

In 1993, the Patuxent Center and the International Crane Foundation began to release whooper chicks from their captive breeding program in Florida to form a resident wild whooping crane flock.

The habitat chosen for the Florida flock is a mixture of freshwater marsh, pastures, and agricultural grain fields. There are plenty of nesting places in the marsh and lots of food in the fields.

The whooper chicks are placed in the Florida flock when they're about a year old. When the chicks first arrive, they're kept in large pens placed in the flock habitat. Half the pen has marsh habitat, while the other half has a drier field habitat. After 2 weeks, the pens are opened, and the birds are free to leave. Within a few weeks, all the cranes are moving about in their new habitat.

In Florida, a biologist works with young whooping cranes. These cranes will soon be released to form a wild resident flock.

Some whooping cranes spend most of their lives in captivity (left). But biologists are working hard to establish new flocks, like these Florida whooping cranes (below). They have been released from captivity to form a wild resident whooping crane flock.

One of the most encouraging signs for biologists is the behavior of the new non-migrating whoopers. They have danced and paired up. They've established territories, mated, and built nests. Biologists hope the flock will produce its own chicks in the next few years.

So far, the flock is doing well. By the fall of 1996, 100 chicks had been placed in the flock over a period of 3 years, and 49 of them were still alive. Thirty more chicks were released into the flock at the end of 1996.

Biologists haven't given up on establishing another wild migrating flock. The Canadian government plans to use whooper chicks from the Calgary Zoo captive breeding program to start another migratory flock in Saskatchewan or Manitoba in Canada.

Kent Clegg uses his ultralight aircraft to teach whoopers how to migrate.

Crane parents teach their chicks how to migrate. To establish another wild migrating flock, biologists will have to be the parents and "teach" the cranes how to migrate. To do this, Kent Clegg, a researcher in Grace, Idaho, has been experimenting with teaching whoopers how to migrate—using an ultralight aircraft.

A newly hatched crane will **imprint,** or attach and bond with, almost the first thing it sees. In this case, the chicks Kent gets from the Patuxent Center imprint on him—they think he's their parent.

The whooper chicks follow Kent about, even flying after him when he goes up in the ultralight aircraft.

So far, Kent's efforts to teach the whoopers to migrate are working. He has successfully led three fall migrations—with three different small flocks of cranes, both sandhills and whoopers—from Grays Lake, Idaho, to Bosque del Apache NWR in New Mexico. Biologists are hoping that these same techniques will allow them to establish other wild migratory whooper flocks.

All of these ongoing efforts to help the whooping cranes are paying off. The annual bird count on November 30, 1997, showed that there were 356 whooping cranes in the world, and that 171 of these had been in the original Wood Buffalo flock. It's not a lot, but it's better than 16!

Whooping cranes aren't out of danger, but American and Canadian biologists are proud of the whoopers' comeback from the brink of extinction. The sad fact is that whooping cranes may never be *out* of danger because their habitat is always *in* danger. Sandhills face the same problem. Most sandhill crane species are not endangered, but their habitat is. If their habitat disappears, sandhills will be gone too.

Power lines, pesticides, wetlands turned into shopping centers and farms, and disease from overcrowding have all reduced the North American crane populations. In addition, no matter how many cranes are raised in captivity, biologists can't bring more diversity back to the whoopers' gene pool. But people can work to protect cranes' wetland habitats so that crane populations never drop so low again. With this continuing help, whoopers and sandhills could be flying over North America for millions of years to come.

GLOSSARY

band: an identification tag attached to an animal that helps biologists keep track of where the animal goes

brooding: warming eggs or young birds in a nest

captive breeding: raising chicks in laboratories

egg tooth: the hard, pointed knob on top of a young chick's beak, used for breaking out of the eggshell. After hatching, this special "tooth" falls off.

endangered: at risk of losing all members of a species forever

extinct: having no members of a species left alive

flock: a group of birds that live together

flyway: an established route that migratory birds take from their wintering grounds to their nesting grounds and back again

gene pool: the collection of all the genes that make up a species

genes: tiny units in the cells of living things that determine the characteristics that offspring will inherit from their parents

habitat: the type of environment in which an animal normally lives

incubating: keeping eggs warm so chicks will develop and hatch

migrate: to move from one location to another, usually to reach new feeding grounds

omnivorous: eating both plants and animals

pip: the first crack a hatching chick makes in the egg

plumage: a bird's covering of feathers

predator: an animal that hunts and kills other animals for food

preen: to clean and smooth the feathers

resident flock: a group of birds that stay in the same area all year long. They do not migrate.

species: a specific kind of animal within a larger scientific grouping of animals with similar traits

territory: an area claimed as one's home and defended from other animals

trachea: a structure in the throat, also called the windpipe

tundra: a treeless area, located in the far north, with many lakes and meadows

wetlands: areas where there is more water than dry land

INDEX

appearance, 10-15; of chicks, 29, 31
Aransas National Wildlife Refuge, 21, 22, 34
archaeopteryx, 8-9

banding, 19-21
beaks, 10, 15, 16, 32
Bosque del Apache National Wildlife Refuge, 21, 22, 37, 40, 44
brooding, 29

Calgary Zoo, 37, 43
captive breeding programs, 36-37, 42–43
caring for young, 10, 29–30, 32
chicks, 29–32; appearance of, 29, 31; diet of, 29, 30; size of, 29
Clegg, Kent, 44

dancing, 26
diet, 15, 16, 29, 30
disease, 40, 45
Drewien, Rod, 37, 38

eggs, 27–28, 29, 30, 36
eyes, 15, 29

family groups, 23, 25
feathers. See plumage
flocks, 23, 38–41, 42–43
flying, 22, 31, 44
flyways, 18, 20, 21, 22, 25, 35, 37
foster parents, 37–40

gene pool, 34–35, 45
Grays Lake National Wildlife Refuge, 21, 37–40, 44

habitat, 17, 18, 20, 27, 42; preserving, 35, 45
hatching, 29

incubation, 28, 37
International Crane Foundation, 37, 42

mating, 10, 14, 26
migration, 18–22, 25, 37, 43, 44

national refuges, 16, 21, 22, 34, 37, 44
nesting grounds, 7, 8, 18, 21, 25–32
nests, 27, 30

Patuxent Wildlife Research Center, 36–37, 38, 39, 42, 44
pipping, 29
plumage, 8, 13–14, 31, 33
power lines, 37, 40, 41, 45
predators, 16, 32, 37, 40
preening, 13–14

sandhill cranes: appearance of, 11, 13–14, 15; as foster parents, 37–40; number of, 10; preening, 13–14; size of, 11; subspecies, 11, 17, 40
saving whoopers, 33–45
size, 10, 11, 12; of chicks, 29
species of cranes, 9

territories, 23–24, 25

voices, 7, 10, 22, 24, 31, 32

wetlands, 17, 18, 20, 33, 37
whooping cranes: appearance of, 14, 15; number of, 33–35, 45; preening, 14; saving, 33–45; size of, 12
wintering grounds, 18, 21, 22, 23–24
Wood Buffalo National Park, 35, 36, 38, 39, 45

ABOUT THE AUTHOR

Lesley A. DuTemple makes her home at the edge of a canyon in Salt Lake City, Utah. She is a writer of both books and magazine articles. She has written four other children's books for the Lerner Group: *Whales, Tigers, Moose,* and *Polar Bears,* all part of the Early Bird Nature Book series. She has done freelance work for numerous magazines and is a regular contributor to *Dolphin Log,* the children's publication of the Costeau Society.

Lesley is a graduate of the University of California. She also did graduate studies for her M.B.A. at the University of Southern California. She lives with her husband, daughter, and son—as well as a dog, two cats, several tropical fish, a resident porcupine, a family of raccoons, and assorted deer.

Photos courtesy of: © Wendy Shattil/Bob Rozinski, front cover, pp. 4-5, 6-7, 10, 19 (left), 22, 26, 41 (right), 45; © Lynn Stone, back cover, pp. 12, 13 (right), 14, 15 (top), 16 (right), 17, 18, 30, 31; © Mary Ann McDonald, p. 2; © Science VU/Visuals Unlimited, p. 8; © Joe McDonald/Visuals Unlimited, pp. 9 (top), 16 (left); U.S. Fish and Wildlife Service/Mimi Westervelt, p. 9 (bottom); © William J. Weber/Visuals Unlimited, pp. 11, 23 (right), 33, 43 (left); © Gil Lopez-Espina/Visuals Unlimited, p. 13 (left); © Arthur Morris/Visuals Unlimited, pp. 15 (bottom), 19 (right), 34; © Marc Epstein/Visuals Unlimited, p. 20; © Rod Drewien, pp. 23 (left), 27, 28 (top), 29, 35, 36 (both), 38 (both), 39, 40-41; © Roger Treadwell/Visuals Unlimited, p. 24; © Ross Frid/Visuals Unlimited, p. 25; © Charlie Heidecker/Visuals Unlimited, p. 28 (bottom); © David J. Books/Visuals Unlimited, p. 32; © Jonathan Male/Patuxent WRC, p. 37; International Crane Foundation, pp. 42, 43 (right); © Kent Clegg, p. 44. Map on p. 21 by Lejla Fazlic Omerovic, copyright © 1999 Carolrhoda Books, Inc.